The Angel at the Bottom of the Garden

With love & blessings

Written and Illustrated by

Julie Ann Heath

potters maze

The First Day

For years I have
gone in and out of the house.

Each day rushing
to and fro.

The sound
of ticking
permanently
in my head.
Work, chores, appointments
and people, each minute accounted for.

...tick... ...tock... ...tick... ...tock...

...tick... ...tock... ...tick... ...tock...

The kneeling angel
at the bottom of
my garden...
...you watch and listen.
You look so serene
and composed.

Watching. Listening. Waiting.
Why am. I talking to you by the way when I'm so late!
And why have I come down to the bottom of the garden in my slippers again!
2
3
4
5

The Second Day

Time.

Everything we do is controlled by time.

What is time?

I know there will be some sort of explanation but that's no good to me.

I was never any good at science.

...but anyway I don't want to understand time, I just want to live with it.

Or maybe I want to live without it?
Time seems to chase after me.
I am trying to push it back on the one hand,
And yet there never seems to be enough of it on the other!

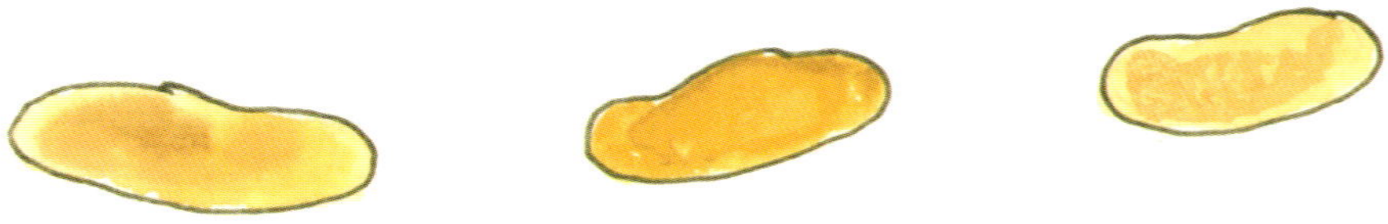

Tuesday
Poor angel you must think that I am talking nonsense.
I wonder if my neighbours can hear me talking to you?
Even more worrying, I wonder if my neighbours can see me in my pyjamas!

You know Angel, when I think about it, life seems to be all about measurements!

LITRE · PINT · GLASS · BOTTLE · MUG · METRE · YARD · FOOT · CENTIMETRE

ONE POUND · FIVE POUNDS · TEN POUNDS · TWENTY POUNDS · FIFTY POUNDS · THOUSAND · TEN THOUSAND

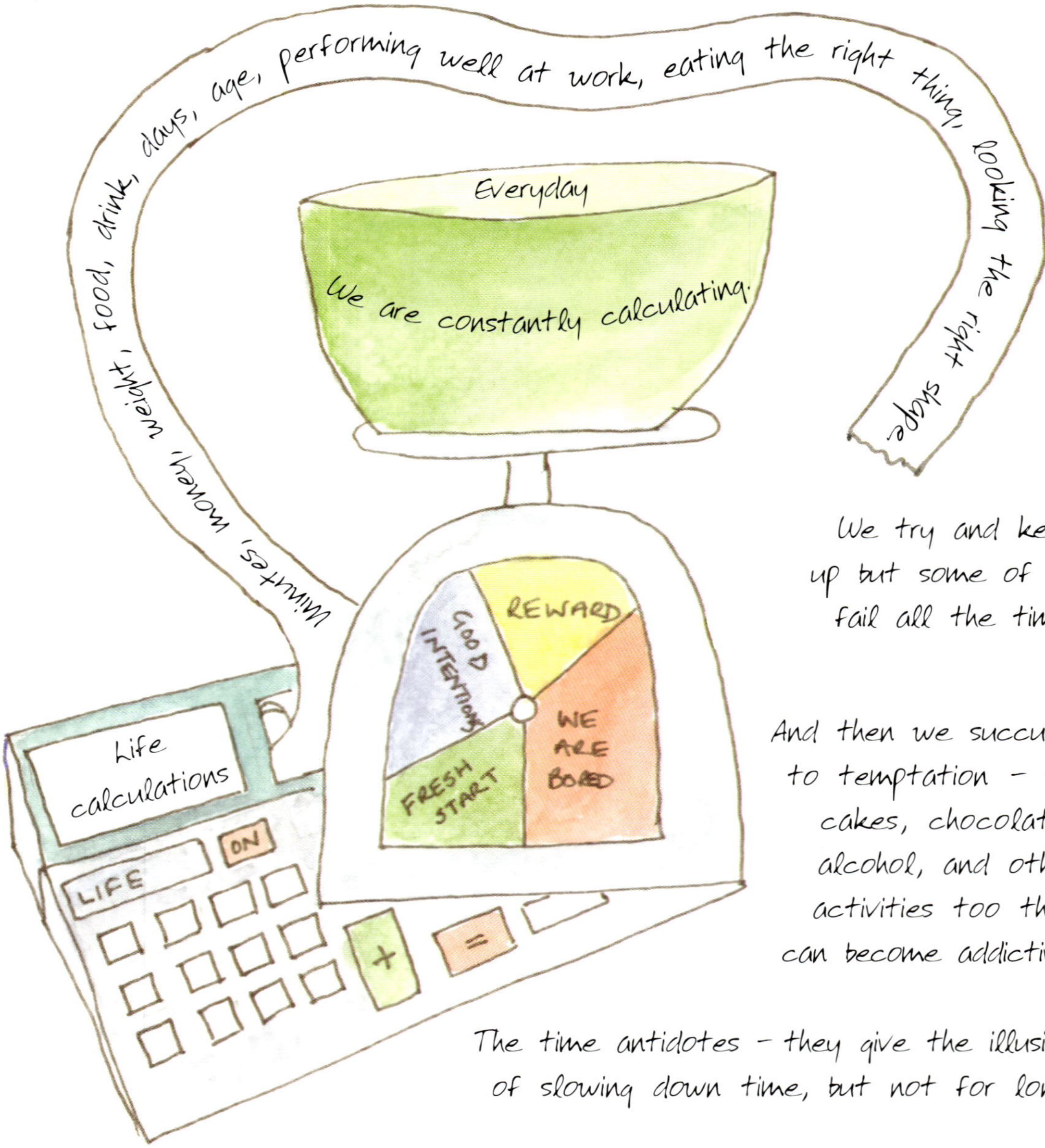

We try and keep up but some of us fail all the time!

And then we succumb to temptation – to cakes, chocolate, alcohol, and other activities too that can become addictive.

The time antidotes – they give the illusion of slowing down time, but not for long!

And then it's time for bed, and then back on the cycle, that's the work cycle, life cycle, the calculation cycle not bicycle; mind you I have one of those – a bicycle I mean.

WEEK · DAY · MONTH · YEAR · MINUTE · SECOND · HOUR · POUND · KILO · STONE · CUP ·

· MILLION · BYTES · MEGA BYTES · CALORIES · FAT CONTENT · SUGAR · SALT . . .

My bicycle is in the garage out of sight – If I see it I will have to use it! It is not only a bicycle, but it is also a shame cycle!

CAFE
CHOCOLATE
STONES
KILOS
WEEK ONE
WEEK TWO
WEEK THREE
WEEK FOUR
SALARY SCALE
£75K
£100K
£150K
£250K
£500K
£1000
£2000
£3000
£4000
£5000
£7000
£8000
£10000
£12000
£15000
£17000
£20000
£25000
£30000
£40000
£50000
BMI
TEENAGER
GYM TOP
HAIR DYE
NIGHT CREAM
DAY CREAM
EYE
TEEN'S
20's
30's
40's
50's
60's
70's
80's

The Third Day
WORK
DYE
Check on Dad
DEFROST
PACK LUNCH
PETROL
MOT
GIRLS NIGHT
VITAMINS
BANK STATEMENT
POLISH
DOG
CAT
DOG
CAT
CEREAL

Angel,
Have you ever wondered why we sleep? Well you don't of course Angel. Well, you might? Why do we sleep? For rest and relaxation I suppose. After all we are not machines. There is a special time before sleep when we unwind and calm down. As a child I would read a book, or I was told a story, but now I use that time to check things off my 'to do list' to see how well I have done.
The pillow has become a 'to do pillow'.
Sad isn't it.
DAILY SUCCESS CHART
HIGH ACHIEVER
IMPRESSIVE
ADMIRED
DOING ALRIGHT
KEEPING PACE
BELOW PAR

The Third Night

Sleeptime...

It should of course be a time for dreaming but life has become so complex, do we have time for dreams anymore?

Usually, we are too busy thinking about what we have to do tomorrow.

Nightmares and hallucinations!
Now we seem to have time for them.
That wave of negativity which sweeps over you in the early hours!
That has to be pushed back too, just like time!

Do angels suffer from anxiety I wonder?
You don't look like you do - but then neither do most of us!
I know Angel - I worry you don't I?
Is that why you pray?

The Fourth Day

Nothing to wear! Another thought which I am sure doesn't enter your head Angel! Of course we do have clothes to wear! Well most of us anyway.

First impressions you see! It's time again! We can't wait to get to know someone so we try and guess what they are like from the garments they are wearing! And trust me clothes lie!

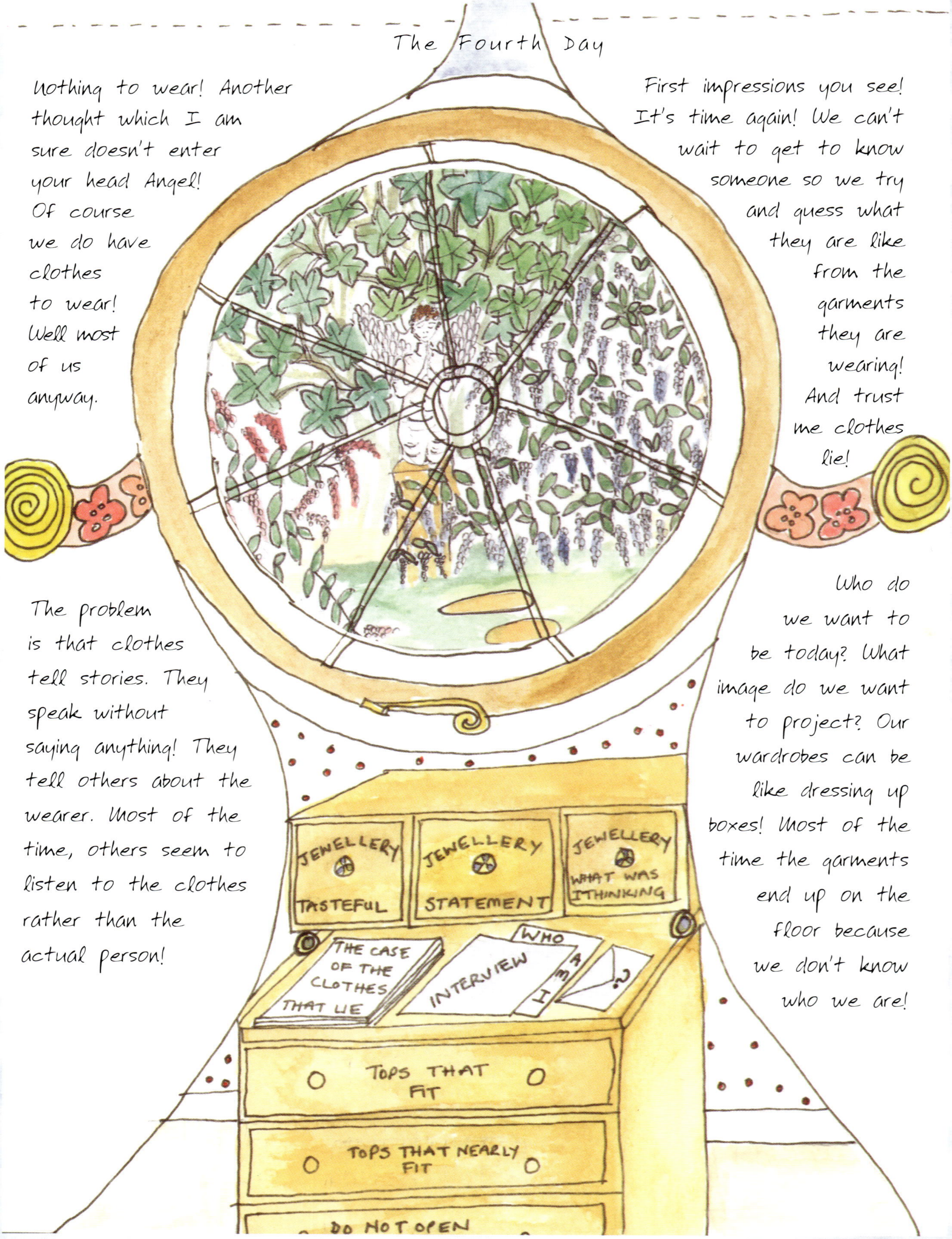

The problem is that clothes tell stories. They speak without saying anything! They tell others about the wearer. Most of the time, others seem to listen to the clothes rather than the actual person!

Who do we want to be today? What image do we want to project? Our wardrobes can be like dressing up boxes! Most of the time the garments end up on the floor because we don't know who we are!

DRESSING UP
Who do I want to be?
I have Nothing to wear
SEXY
Too Thin
Too short
Too old
Too formal
Too casual
Too young
Too Tight
Too boring
Too fat

PROFESSIONAL
BUSINESS
TOO MANLY ?
COSY:
WARM:-
SAD?
TOO TIGHT?
ELEGANT:
TOO BORING?
SHORT: SHARP:
HIDES EVERY THING!
CLASSIC:
SEXY : TOO TARTY?
COMFORTABLE!
CASUAL: PREDICTABLE!
TOO POINTY!
PRETTY: GIRLY: TOO OLD?
... arms ?
WHO SHALL I BE 2DAY?
A CARDIGAN?
TOO COSY?
TOO HIGH!
WILL GET TOO DIRTY ?
CAN'T WALK IN THEM
LOVE IT : NEVER WEAR IT

We are like actors and actresses.
We dress for a part!
But what is our part? Who tells us?
And do we get to choose?
Ideally, my part would be in a romantic comedy, a happy ending.
However I suspect the reality is a bit more like a farce or a pantomime.
THIS YEAR'S PANTOMINE
BABES WOMEN
IN THE
HUMAN WOOD
RESOURCES DEPT
DRESSING UP BOX
And Angel, who knows how it will end?
SCRIPT
URGENT
To/ YOU
SENDER:- ADDRESS UNKNOWN
ACTOR:- STOP!
ACTRESS:- THE POLICE ARE CHASING YOU
ACTOR:- (STOLE AN ICE CREAM VAN!)
ACTRESS:- WHY?
ACTOR:- BECAUSE IT'S SUNDAE
ACTRESS:- (LAUGHS)
ACTOR:- TO FIND YOU
ACTRESS:- (SMILES)
THE END
ACTOR:- WAS THAT THE END?
ACTRESS:- SURELY NOT
I certainly don't!

MOODY
The Fifth Day
Do you remember teenage wishes? How they were extraordinary wishes! What did I want you may ask? What do any of us want? A life permanently lived on a 'red carpet'? To be rich and famous? Yes please!
I was day dreaming. What do you see Angel? Glasses with short measures? Or space for more?
Love and friendship.
Being popular is what it is all about! Well, I thought so back then anyway!
How moody?
I think maybe it depends on the nature of the person don't you?
RICH FAMOUS POPULAR
LOVED RICH FAMOUS
That was me when I didn't quite achieve my 'Hollywood' lifestyle.
So there it is, a picture of wishes. And now the reality!
Some of us mourn what is absent whilst others delight in what they have.
Well the glass of life can look decidedly.
Half empty if we compare it to those wishes.
Has life been a 'short measure' so far?
A BOTTLE OF WISHES?

Friday
True
One's
SHOES
CLOTHES
HOME

The Sixth Day
Saturday

Love!

Love!

Love!

Love is the answer?

Well I didn't find love last night,
so still no answer!

When we think
we have found
love anyway there
are always those
that try and
burst our bubble.

...and our hearts are so fragile.

From what I can see, most of
us have repaired hearts anyway.

Some with patches, others with stitches.

Some have hearts that are still coming
undone and the stuffing is all falling out!

Obviously this is just picture language, metaphors for
shattered emotions and painful experiences.

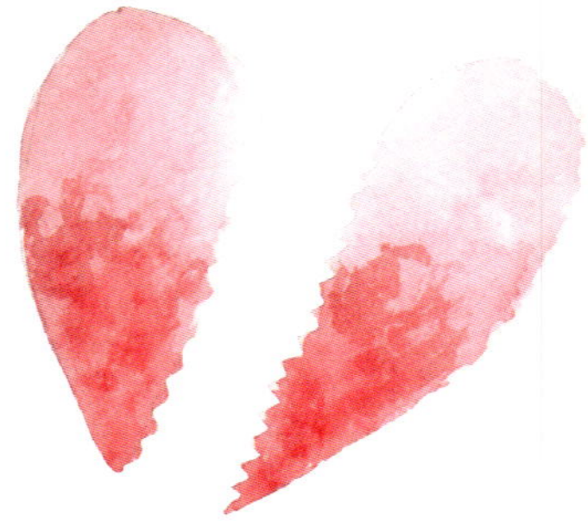

And why do we take so long to repair?

And the heartbreaking memories - what about those?

We try and hide them out of sight,
but unexpectedly they come out from nowhere.

It is those memories that tend to run down
my face, they are the clear, wet and salty type.

And yet Angel,
we keep on pursuing love.
I am being thoughtful again.
Some say we are made for love, don't they?
But what else could we be made for?
Relationships are so hard and yet so wonderful!
To be accepted totally and unconditionally for whom we are!
Wow! That is the greatest gift we can be given in life!
It totally repairs any broken heart and fulfils our dreams.
In return, we must do the same for the other.
And sadly that is where the problem can arise.
How long are we expected to keep each other happy?
Is it really for a life time?
What can we do Angel?
What's the formula
for love?

The Seventh Day

Hello Angel, I am not in a rush today.
By the way it's my birthday!
normally I dread my birthdays but not today.
I have talked to you so much recently.
I am so glad you are here.
you are such a good listener.

You have been patiently watching
and listening to me this whole time.
And you pray? Praying – is it like talking?

Well, I have decided that it's time to
dream again. I'm not too old am I?
Surely there is always time for dreams,
but who do you share them with?

I have made new dreams.
I have woven them into a flying carpet,
as dreams should always be able to fly don't you think?
Can you see Angel?
This time I will share them just like you.

Angel, do you have to kneel?
I wish the ground wasn't so wet!
My pyjamas will be so muddy!
I do hope I can get up again.
My knees are not what they used to be!

...so how do you hold your hands Angel?

Electricity

Sally Morgan and Pauline Lalor

WHY WASTE IT?

SIMON & SCHUSTER
YOUNG BOOKS

This book has been prepared for
Simon & Schuster Young Books by
Globe Enterprises of Nantwich, Cheshire

Design: M&M Design Partnership
Photographs: Ecoscene except
ZEFA (7)

First published in Great Britain in1993
by Simon & Schuster Young Books
Campus 400, Maylands Avenue
Hemel Hempstead, Herts HP2 7EZ

Printed and bound in Singapore
by Kim Hup Lee Printing Co Pte Ltd

A catalogue record for this book is
available from the British Library
ISBN 0 7500 1410 5

Contents

We use electricity every day	6–7
Electricity is a type of energy	8–9
Electricity is dangerous	10–11
Power stations	12–13
Delivering electricity	14–15
Wasting electricity	16–17
Batteries store electricity	18–19
Can electricity be recycled?	20–21
Fewer power stations	22–23
Saving the countryside	24–25
New ways with electricity	26–27
How can we save it?	28–29
Index	30–31

We use electricity every day

Our lives would be very different without electricity.

We need it to light our houses and schools. In many homes, people use electricity for cooking and heating. It also powers our televisions, stereo systems and computers. Even some trains are electric.

How many electrical things do you use each day?

Sucr

Electricity is a type of energy

We cannot see electricity. We can only see what it does.

When an electric fire is switched on, first we see a red glow and then we feel its warmth. In some way, electricity has turned into heat and light.

Heat and light are both forms of energy, so is electricity. Electricity can change into several different types of energy. Can you name any?

Electricity is dangerous

You must be careful with electricity. It can run through your body like a flash of lightning giving you an electric shock.

Electrical things are safe as long as you use them properly.

You must never push anything except a plug into an electric socket and you must keep electrical things away from water.

Power stations

Electricity is made in power stations where fuels such as coal, oil and gas are burnt to produce heat.

The heat turns water into steam. The steam then passes through a turbine which spins round making electricity.

Delivering electricity

Electricity made in power stations is carried across the countryside to the factories and homes that use it.

It travels along thick metal wires, called power lines. These are held high above the ground by tall pylons.

Most homes have a meter that measures how much electricity is used. Ask an adult to help you read your meter.

Wasting electricity

We often waste electricity because we don't switch things off.

City streets and shops stay lit all night when most of us are asleep. We leave lights on in empty rooms in our homes. Sometimes we leave electrical things running when we are not using them.

How do you waste electricity?

Batteries store electricity

If you put a battery into a torch it becomes part of an electric circuit. When the torch is switched on the chemicals inside the battery make electricity which lights the bulb.

When the electricity is used up, the battery is thrown away. Some batteries can be recharged and used again.

What things do you use that have batteries?

POLICE
abc

Delco General
POMPEY TYRE SERVICES
P.T.S
FULLY GUARANTEED
MONARCH
MARATHON

Can electricity be recycled?

Paper, metal and glass can all be reused. They can be recycled and used again.

Once electricity is used, it turns into heat, light, sound or movement, and is lost for ever. The only way we can save electricity, is to use less of it.

You can recycle your old batteries. Some towns have collection points. What do you do with your old batteries?

New ways with electricity

There are ways of making electricity without burning coal, gas and oil. Running water, wind and even the heat and light from the sun can all be used.

We still need the power stations because we can't make all our electricity using new ways. But we save fuel, make less acid rain and dig fewer holes in the ground.

Index

acid rain 22, 26

batteries 18, 21

bulb 18, 29

coal 24, 26

cooking 6

electric circuit 18

electric fire 9

electric shock 10

electric socket 10

energy 9, 29

fuels 12, 22, 26